AF589711

Practise writing the letters in the big letters above. Start at the dot.
Then practise them below:

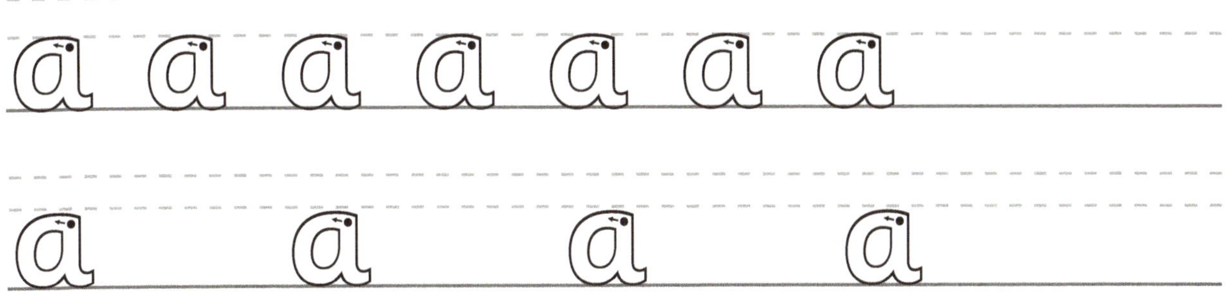

Find and circle the pictures which begin with the 'a' sound (as in 'ant'):

Circle all of the letter a.

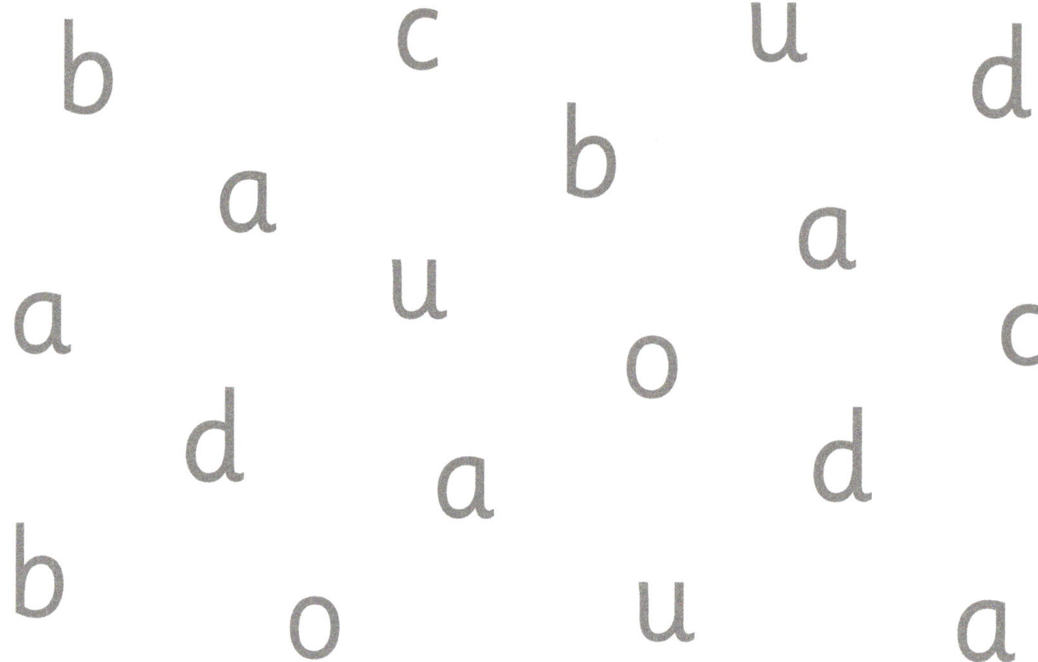


Join the pictures which begin with the same sounds. See the example.

Practise writing the letters in the big letters above. Start at the dot.
Then practise them below:

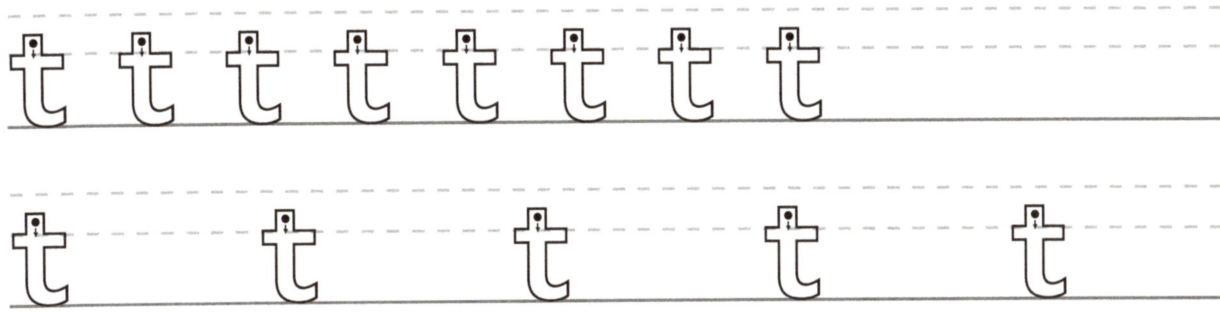

Find and circle the pictures which begin with the 't' sound (as in 'top'):

## Reading Practice

This is a cat.

This is a hat.

This is a dog.

This is a mat.

## Words we know

a a a

at at at

cat cat cat

# Colour the pictures

cat hat mat

rat bat fat

Circle the picture which does not rhyme.

cat mat dog hat

## Numbers

Write these numbers and then colour them in.

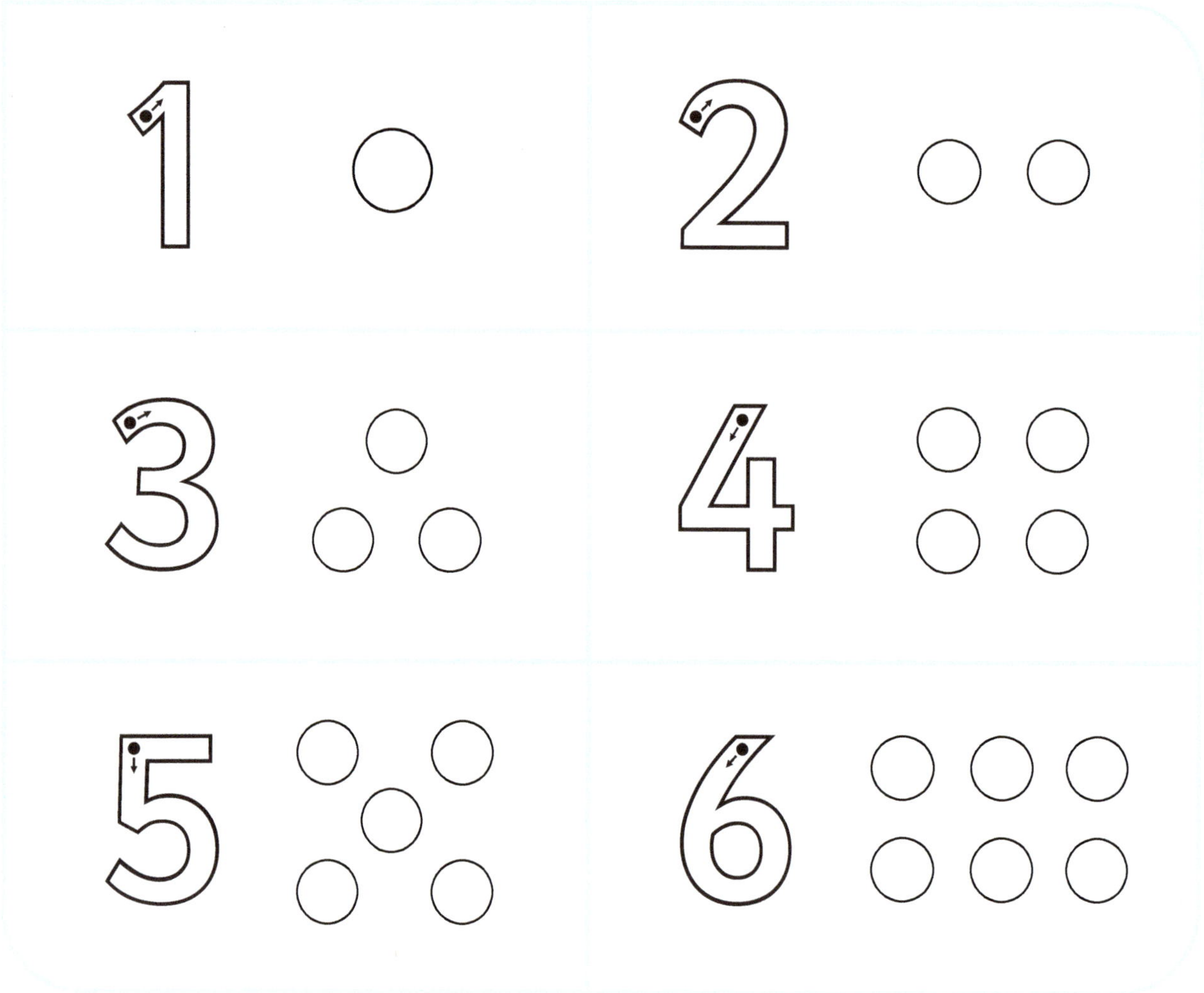

| | |
|---|---|
| 1 | 2 |
| 3 | 4 |
| 5 | 6 |

## Teacher Feedback

Practise writing the letters in the big letters above. Start at the dot.
Then practise them below:

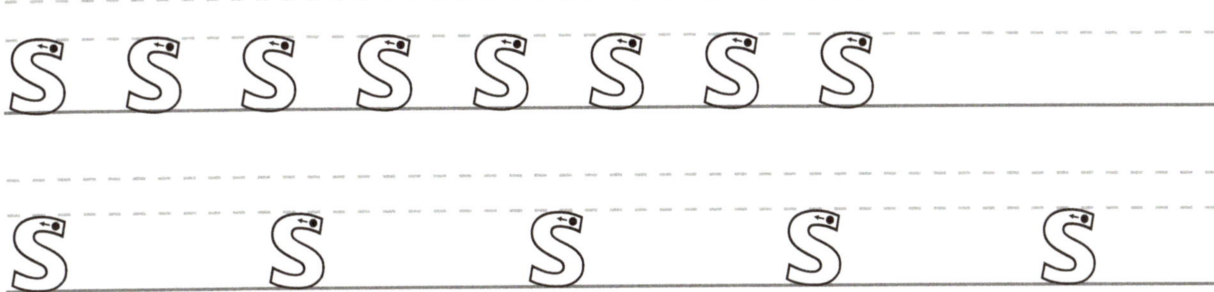

Find and circle the pictures which begin with the 's' sound (as in 'sit'):

## Words we can read

Practise reading these words.  Try and think of a sentence for each word.

| | | | |
|---|---|---|---|
| sat | at | This | as |
| is | a | the | cat |

Circle the picture which does not rhyme.

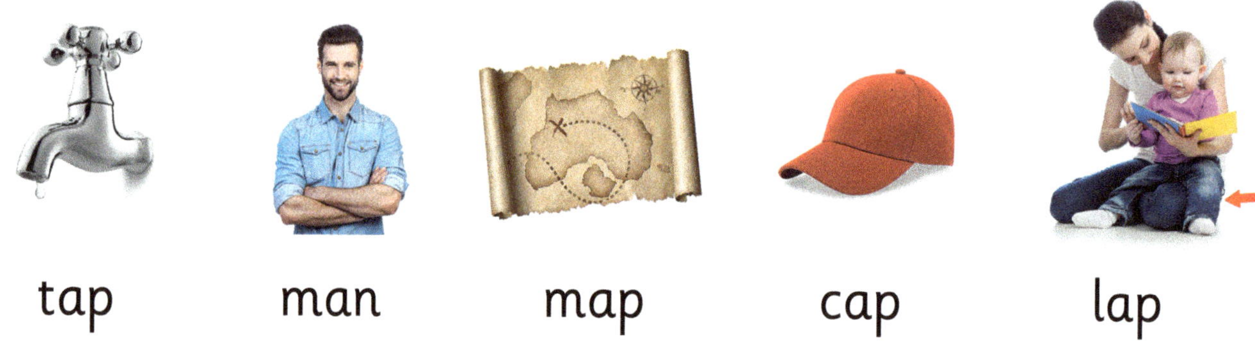

tap  man  map  cap  lap

## Find the right letters

Say the sound of the letter in the box. Then circle all the letters which are the same.

## Reading Practice

This is a girl.

This is a boy.

This is a cat.

This is a dog.

## Words we know

at at at

sat sat sat

is is is

## Numbers

Write these numbers:

1 2 3 4 5 6

## Teacher Feedback

Practise writing the letters in the big letters above. Start at the dot.
Then practise them below:

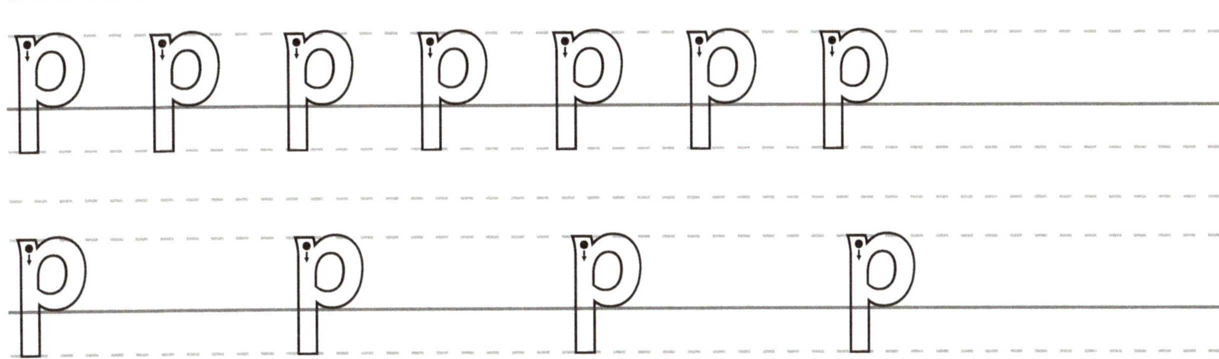

Find and circle the pictures which begin with the 'p' sound (as in 'pat'):

## Words we can read

Practise reading these words. Try and think of a sentence for each word.

| This | Pippa | cat | Sam |
|---|---|---|---|
| pat | tap | is | dog |
| boy | the | sat | girl |

Now see if you can label the pictures.

Circle the two pictures which begin with the same sound.

## Reading Practice

This is Pippa.

This is Sam the cat.

This is a tap.

Pat the dog.

## Words we know

pat pat pat

tap tap tap

the the the

Colour the letter in. Then circle the pictures with the 's' sound.

6

## Reading Practice

Practise these words with your teacher. Then read the sentences.

| Pippa | girl | This | Sam |
|---|---|---|---|
| Pippa's | is | cat | a |

This is Pippa. Pippa is a girl.

This is Sam. Sam is a cat.

Sam is Pippa's cat.

## Your sentence

Finish the sentence with a word from the box. Then draw a picture for your sentence.

cat dog boy girl tap

## Numbers

Write these sums and practise reading them.

1 •
2 ••
3 •••
4 ••••
5 •••••
6 ••••••

1 + 1 = 2

2 + 3 = 5

4 + 1 = 5

3 + 3 = 6

2 + 2 = 4

## Teacher Feedback

Practise writing the letters in the big letters above. Start at the dot.
Then practise them below:

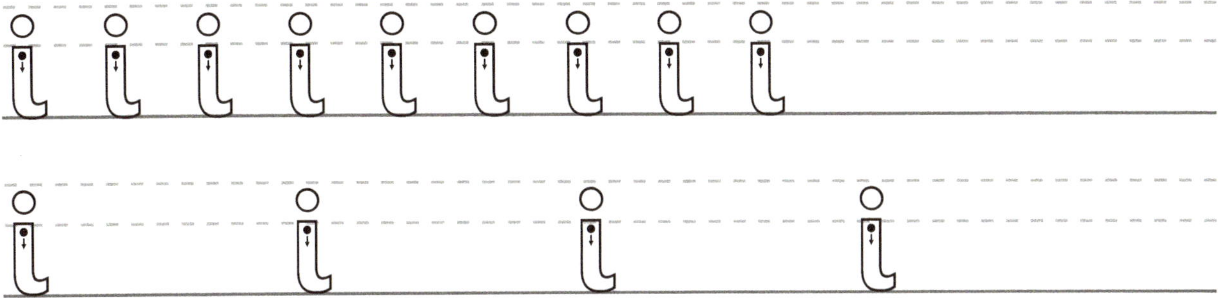

Find and circle the pictures which begin with the 'i' sound (as in 'it'):

Colour the letter in. Then circle the pictures with the 'i' sound.

## Words we can read

Practise reading these words. Try and think of a sentence for each word.

| | | | |
|---|---|---|---|
| This | Pippa | cat | Sam |
| pat | tap | is | dog |
| boy | the | sat | girl |

## Rhyming

Circle the picture which does not rhyme with the others. The words are on the right. Practise reading them.

bin
pin
tin
van
fin

## Tricky Word to practise

the the the

## Label the pictures

Think about the sounds and fill in the missing letters.

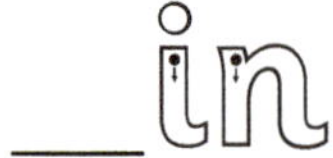

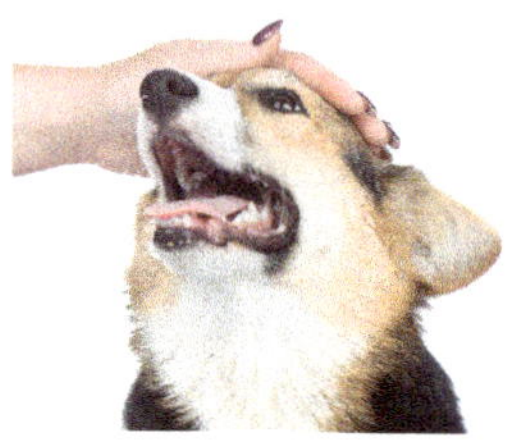

__in c__ __ __it p__ __

## Words we know

the the the

is is is

sit sit sit

## Find the right letters

Say the sound of the letter in the box. Then circle all the letters which are the same.

p q g p q g p

## Reading Practice

Practise these words with your teacher. Then read the sentences.

| cat | the | dog | name | His |
|---|---|---|---|---|
| He | good | is | Sam | Ben |

This is a dog. His name is Ben.

He is a good dog.

This is the cat. His name is Sam.

Now see if you can label the pictures.

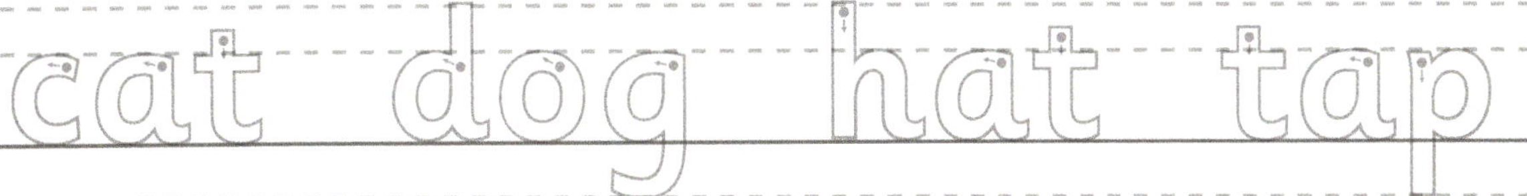

## Numbers

Write these sums and see if you can fill in the missing answers.

1 ●
2 ●●
3 ●●●
4 ●●●●
5 ●●●●●
6 ●●●●●●

2 + 4 = 6

1 + 3 = 4

3 + 2 = ______

1 + 2 = ______

2 + 2 = ______

## Teacher Feedback

______________________________

______________________________

______________________________

## Reading Practice

Arin is a boy.

Pippa is a girl.

This is Arin's dad.

This is Arin's mum.

## Words we know

dad dad dad

sit sit sit

is is is

## Colour the pictures

girl boy ball

## Letter Practice

a a a

s s s

p p p

t t t

Practise writing the letters in the big letters above. Start at the dot. Then practise them below:

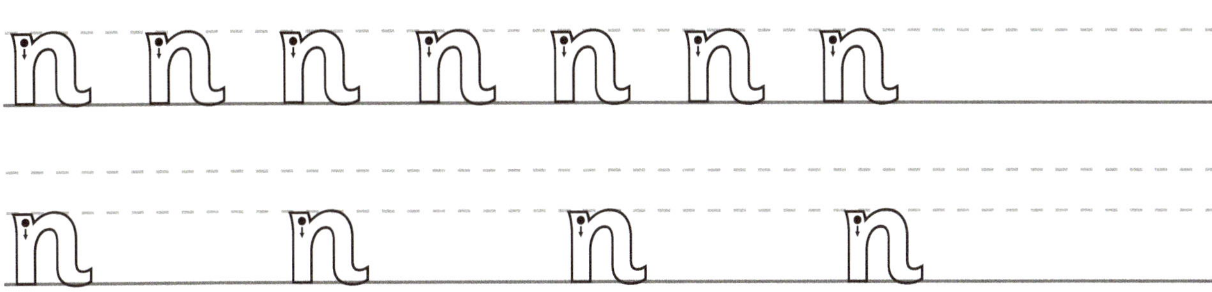

Find and circle the pictures which begin with the 'n' sound (as in 'nest'):

## Find the word

Write the word which goes on each line.

## Find the right letters

Say the sound of the letter in the box. Then circle all the letters which are the same.

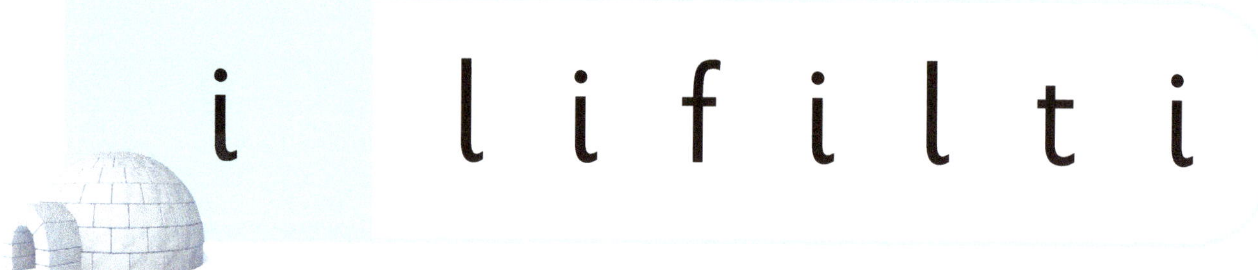


## Words we know

this this this

am am am

pan pan pan

## Numbers

Read these numbers and then colour them in.

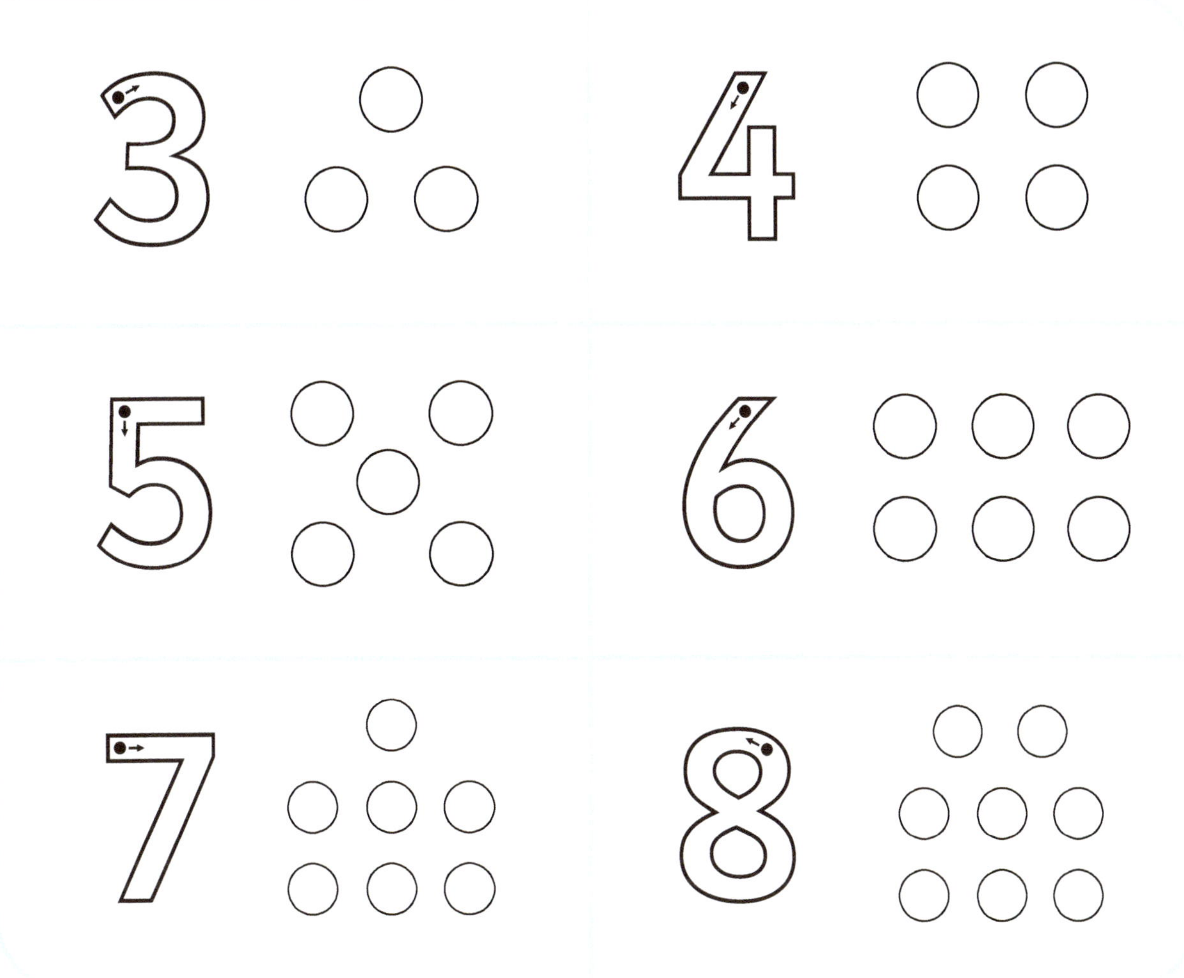


Circle the picture which does not rhyme.

log pig wig dig

## Words we can read

Practise reading these words. Try and think of a sentence for each word.

| | | | |
|---|---|---|---|
| tin | pan | I | sit |
| name | tan | tip | am |
| tap | my | pin | nip |

Circle the pictures which **end** in a 'd' sound.

## Tricky Words to practise

me me me

my my my

## Reading Practice

Practise these words with your teacher. Then read the sentences.

| me | This | I | am | boy | Ben |
|---|---|---|---|---|---|
| My | Arin | is | name | like | dog |

This is me. I am a boy.

My name is Arin. Ben is my dog.

I like Ben.

## About you

Finish the sentence. Get a teacher to help you write your name.

Then draw a picture.

This is me.

My name is

## Choose the word

Some of these are new words, but you can work them out. Circle the right word for each picture.

| | |
|---|---|
| pin<br>pan | nip<br>nap |
| dog<br>bog | pips<br>sips |
| tap<br>lap | hot<br>hat |
| tin<br>tan | cat<br>bat |

## Teacher Feedback

Practise writing the letters in the big letters above. Start at the dot.
Then practise them below:

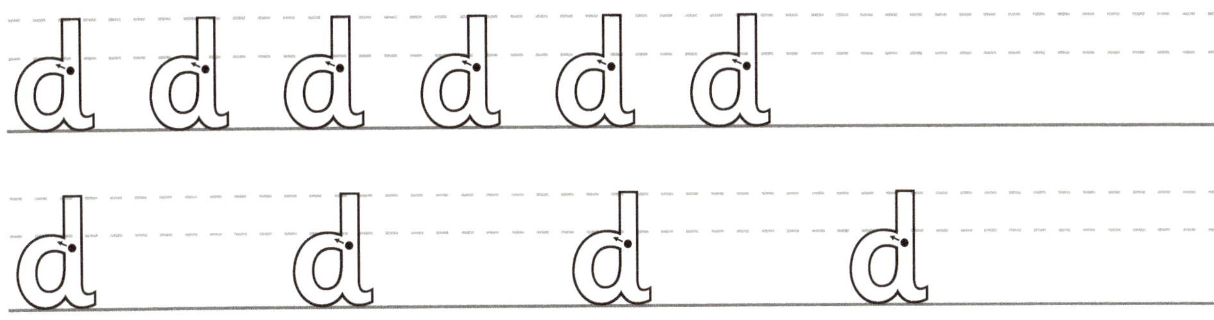

Find and circle the pictures which begin with the 'd' sound (as in 'dot'):

## Numbers

Write these numbers:

3 4 5 6 7 8

| | | | |
|---|---|---|---|
| ________ | ● ● ●<br>● ● ● | ________ | ● ●<br>● ● |
| ________ | ●<br>● ● | ________ | ●<br>● ● ●<br>● ● ● |
| ________ | ● ●<br>●<br>● ● | ________ | ● ●<br>● ● ●<br>● ● ● |

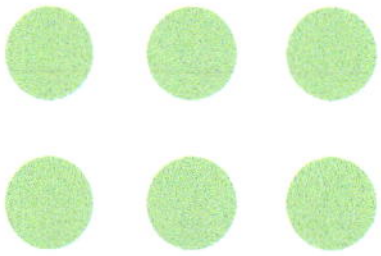

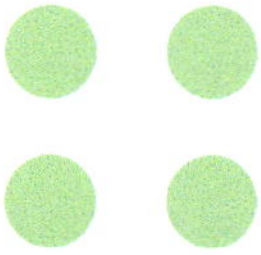

Circle the picture which does not rhyme.

dog log frog boy

## Words we can read

Practise reading these words. Try and think of a sentence for each word.

| | | | |
|---|---|---|---|
| and | did | my | din |
| good | dip | pan | add |
| nip | pin | sit | the |

Circle the pictures which **end** in the 't' sound.

## Tricky Words to practise

and and and

am am am

## Match the letters

Join the lower case and upper case letters together and write them on the line.

| | | |
|---|---|---|
| a | a A | T |
| p | | I |
| s | | P |
| i | | A |
| t | | N |
| n | | D |
| d | | S |

## Reading Practice

Practise these words with your teacher. Then read the sentences.

| girl | Pippa | her | is | cat |
|---|---|---|---|---|
| the | not | good | This | Sam |

This is the girl. Her name is Pippa.

Sam is her cat. Sam is not a good cat.

## True or false?

Read the sentences and tick the right box. You might have to read the story again.

| | True | False |
|---|---|---|
| 1. The girl's name is Pippa. | ○ | ○ |
| 2. Sam is a good cat. | ○ | ○ |

## Label the pictures

Think about the sounds and fill in the missing letters.

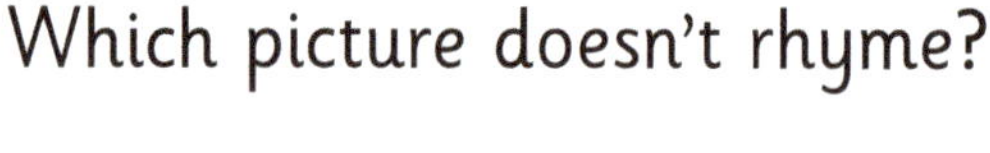

Which picture doesn't rhyme?

## Find the right letters

Say the sound of the letter in the box. Then circle all the letters which are the same.

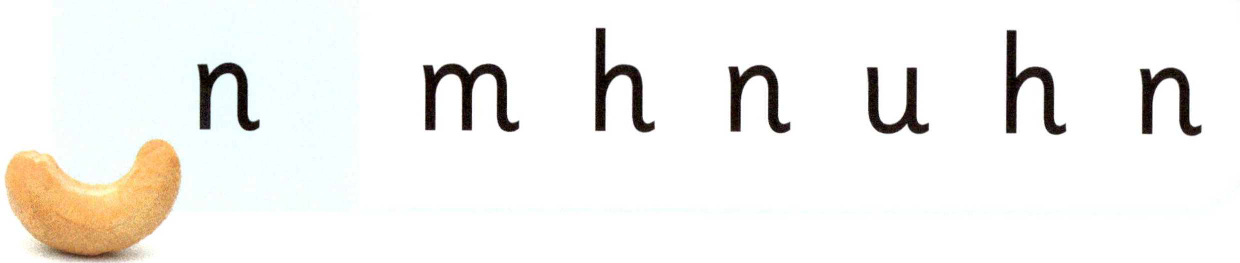

Practise writing the letters in the big letters above. Start at the dot.
Then practise them below:

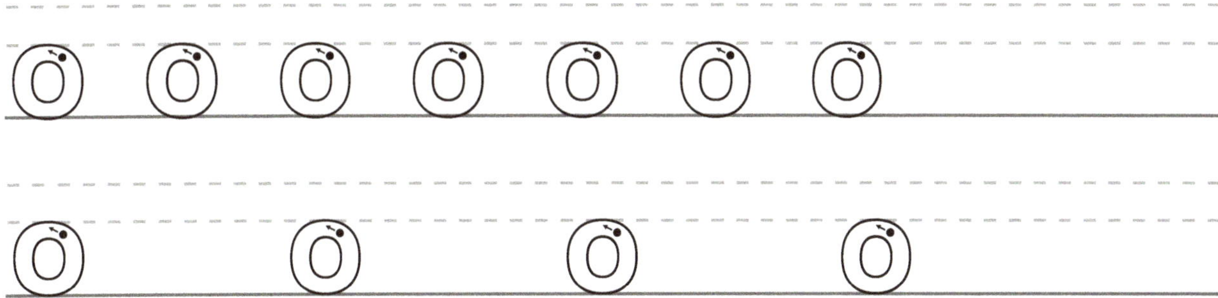

Find and circle the pictures which begin with the 'o' sound (as in 'odd'):

Colour the letter in. Then circle the pictures with the 'o' sound.

## Words we can read

Practise reading these words. Try and think of a sentence for each word.

| not | play | dot | top |
|---|---|---|---|
| like | and | nod | dip |
| sad | the | boy | cat |

Circle the picture which doesn't rhyme.

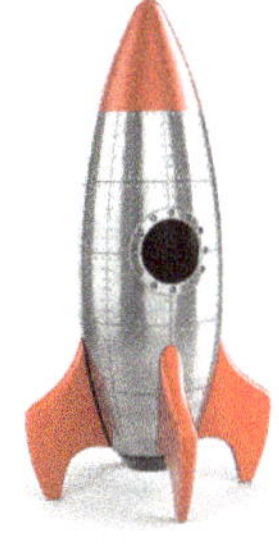

## Label the pictures

Think about the sounds and fill in the missing letters.

## Find the word

Write the word which goes on each line.

## Find the right letters

Say the sound of the letter in the box. Then circle all the letters which are the same.

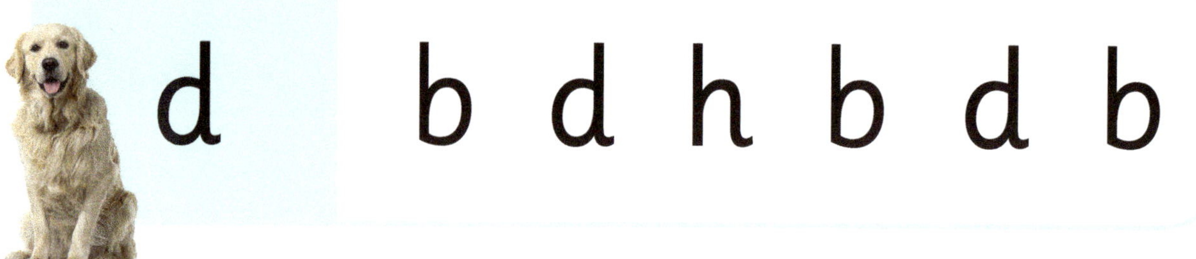


## Words we know

not not not

top top top

and and and

## Reading Practice

Practise these words with your teacher. Then read the sentences.

garden This like play to

with in and Ben likes

This is the garden.

I like to play in the garden with Pippa.

Pippa likes to play in the garden.

Ben and Sam like to play in the garden.

Now see if you can label the pictures.

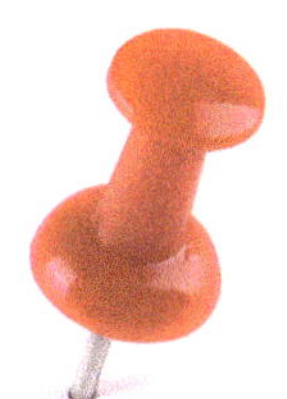

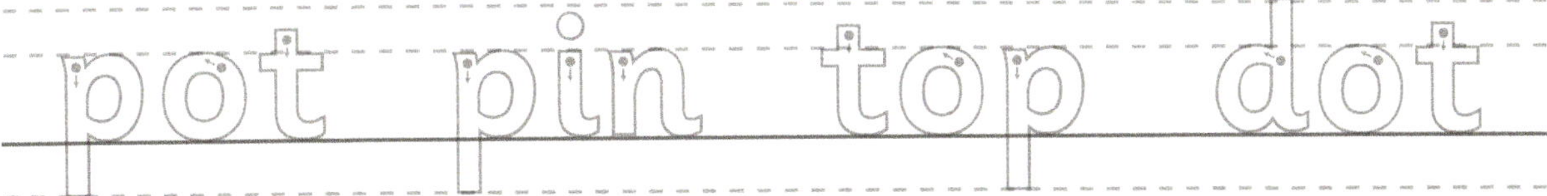

## Numbers

Write these sums and practise reading them.

1 2 3 4 5 6 7 8

4 + 4 = 8

3 + 4 = 7

6 + 2 = 8

2 + 5 = 7

1 + 7 = 8

## Teacher Feedback

## Colour by Numbers

Look at the numbers below and colour in the picture.

1 2 3

4 5

## Practise writing these words

at at at

sat sat sat

as as as

pat pat pat

tap tap tap

is is is

sit sit sit

pit pit pit

# Practise writing these words

sits sits sits

an an an

tan tan tan

tin tin tin

pan pan pan

pin pin pin

nip nip nip

in in in

## Practise writing these words

dad dad dad

sad sad sad

dip dip dip

not not not

on on on

dot dot dot

add add add

top top top

## Space for your own words

Make sure you can write your name.

My name is

I am                    years old.

I like

## Things I can do

Tick these off when you can do them.

| | Yes! |
|---|---|
| I can write my first name. | |
| I can say the alphabet. | |
| I can count to 10. | |
| I know my numbers 1 - 8. | |
| I can say all the days of the week. | |

| | Know sound | Write letter | | Know sound | Write letter |
|---|---|---|---|---|---|
| a | | | A | | |
| t | | | T | | |
| s | | | S | | |
| p | | | P | | |
| i | | | I | | |
| n | | | N | | |
| d | | | D | | |
| o | | | O | | |

**Awesome! Well done!**

# Words I can read

Tick the words you can read without any help.

| Word | Check 1 | Check 2 | Word | Check 1 | Check 2 | Word | Check 1 | Check 2 |
|---|---|---|---|---|---|---|---|---|
| the | | | I | | | play | | |
| cat | | | am | | | by | | |
| dog | | | my | | | with | | |
| girl | | | has | | | Tom | | |
| this | | | name | | | did | | |
| Pippa | | | This | | | in | | |
| Sam | | | Arin | | | sad | | |
| a | | | mum | | | not | | |
| his | | | dad | | | top | | |
| and | | | like | | | add | | |
| Ben | | | his | | | likes | | |
| good | | | her | | | they | | |
| me | | | My | | | are | | |
| in | | | sits | | | have | | |

# Word Race Words

This is a selection of the phonic patterns and key words taught in this workbook as spelling words. Start checking words once the learner has completed Unit 5. Any words needing extra reinforcement should be taught using the 3,3,3 Method and entered into Word Race.

| Word | Check 1 | Check 2 | Word | Check 1 | Check 2 | Word | Check 1 | Check 2 |
|---|---|---|---|---|---|---|---|---|
| at | | | pan | | | pot | | |
| sat | | | pin | | | pats | | |
| as | | | nip | | | | | |
| pat | | | in | | | | | |
| tap | | | and | | | | | |
| is | | | did | | | | | |
| sit | | | dad | | | | | |
| pit | | | sad | | | | | |
| tip | | | dip | | | | | |
| sip | | | not | | | | | |
| sits | | | on | | | | | |
| an | | | dot | | | | | |
| tan | | | add | | | | | |
| tin | | | top | | | | | |

# Word Race

Re-check

START

# Word Race

FINISH

| | | | | | | Re-check |
|---|---|---|---|---|---|---|
| | | | | | | |
| | | | | | | |
| | | | | | | |
| | | | | | | |
| | | | | | | |
| | | | | | | |
| | | | | | | |
| | | | | | | |
| | | | | | | |
| | | | | | | |
| | | | | | | |
| | | | | | | |
| | | | | | | |
| | | | | | | |
| | | | | | | |
| | | | | | | |

www.ingramcontent.com/pod-product-compliance
Ingram Content Group UK Ltd.
Pitfield, Milton Keynes, MK11 3LW, UK
UKHW060020300726
14090UKWH00020B/1081

9 780987 660534